YA
362.299
KIMLAN

APR 1 2 2012

COYA 3-28

D0457088

39092 08151907 8

Park County Library, Cody, Wyoming

Withdrawn

DRUGS & CONSEQUENCES™

THE TRUTH ABOUT
ECSTASY

LANIE KIMLAN and ANNE ALVERGUE

Park County Library, Cody, Wyoming

ROSEN
PUBLISHING®

New York

Published in 2012 by The Rosen Publishing Group, Inc.
29 East 21st Street, New York, NY 10010

Copyright © 2012 by The Rosen Publishing Group, Inc.

First Edition

All rights reserved. No part of this book may be reproduced in any form
without permission in writing from the publisher, except by a reviewer.

Library of Congress Cataloging-in-Publication Data

Kimlan, Lanie.
The truth about ecstasy/Lanie Kimlan, Anne Alvergue.—1st ed.
    p. cm.—(Drugs & consequences)
Includes bibliographical references and index.
ISBN 978-1-4488-4643-6 (library binding)
1. Ecstasy (Drug)—Juvenile literature. 2. Methamphetamine abuse—
Juvenile literature. 3. Teenagers—Drug use—Juvenile literature. I. Alvergue,
Anne. II. Title.
HV5822.M38K56 2012
362.29'9—dc22

2010049936

Manufactured in the United States of America

CPSIA Compliance Information: Batch #S11YA: For further information, contact Rosen Publishing, New York, New York, at 1-800-237-9932.

CONTENTS

INTRODUCTION 4

CHAPTER 1 WHAT IS ECSTASY AND WHAT DOES IT DO? 7

CHAPTER 2 THE HISTORY OF ECSTASY 18

CHAPTER 3 THE RISKS OF ROLLING 28

CHAPTER 4 DRUG USE AND ADDICTION 39

CHAPTER 5 GETTING HELP 48

GLOSSARY 56

FOR MORE INFORMATION 58

FOR FURTHER READING 61

INDEX 62

INTRODUCTION

When fifteen-year-old Sasha Rodriguez and her friend went to the Electric Daisy Carnival, a massive dance party in Los Angeles in June 2010, no one thought that Sasha would be leaving her first rave in an ambulance. And certainly no one thought that the little pill of ecstasy she took would lead to her death. Sasha's friend reported that Sasha quickly began drinking cold water after getting overheated from dancing. Ecstasy can affect the body's ability to replenish electrolytes and Sasha collapsed, hitting her head. Reportedly, when Sasha's friends tried to help her, they were unable to get to her quickly because there were so many people dancing and stepping on them. Sasha was rushed to the intensive care unit of a downtown LA hospital, where she slipped into a coma and experienced multiple organ failure. This is just one account of the very real effects of taking ecstasy.

So what is "ecstasy"? Well, Webster's dictionary defines it as "great joy; rapture; a state of being overpowered with emotion, especially joy; the condition of being beside oneself with feeling." Sounds great, doesn't it? It's also a popular party drug that makes you feel euphoric (happy

Ecstasy is a popular drug that is often taken at large dance parties. The drug often gives users a burst of energy that makes them feel like they can party longer.

and carefree), excited, and confident. But clearly, it has its downside.

MDMA (short for the chemical substance 3,4-methylene-dioxymethamphetamine) is an illegal and expensive drug. Just one hit of MDMA, or ecstasy, can cost between $10 and $30. It has the potential for misuse because it can be psychologically addictive. Ecstasy can cause severe physical and emotional side effects as well. And worst of all, like in the case of Sasha Rodriguez, ecstasy can kill you.

Remember, drugs can seriously hurt you. That's why drug education is helpful. This book explains what ecstasy is, how it affects your body, and what dangerous consequences it can have. You will also learn about addiction and where to go for help if you develop a drug abuse problem.

You have probably heard conflicting messages about drugs. Your parents or teachers may be telling you that drugs are harmful and to just say no, whereas your friends are saying, "Go ahead and try it" because they're supposed to be fun and cool. Do not be confused or misled. Get the facts for yourself. The decision you make could be with you for the rest of your life. It is up to you.

CHAPTER 1

WHAT IS ECSTASY AND WHAT DOES IT DO?

MDMA is a drug that can be known on the street as "ecstasy," "X," "E," or "beans." Drugs are non-food substances that people use to change the way their bodies normally work. For the most part, drugs that have accepted medical uses and no serious side effects are considered legal. Substances such as caffeine and aspirin fall into that category. Alcohol and tobacco are also legal,

7

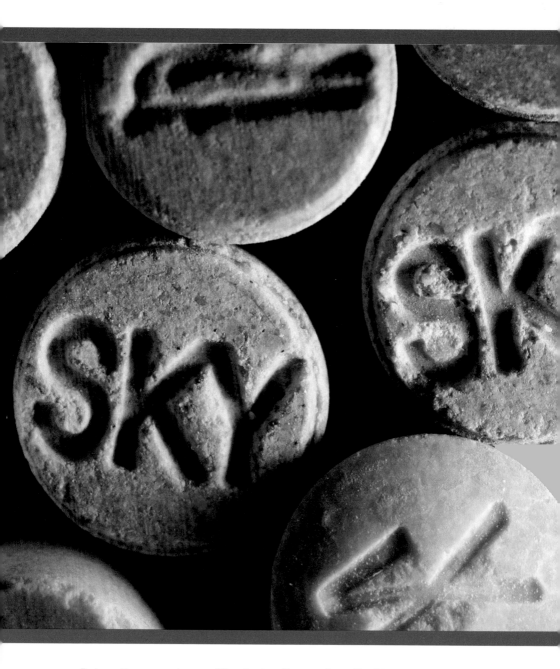

Ecstasy pills can come in many different colors. However, these pills all have two things in common: they have no medical value and are illegal to consume.

but they can be abused. On the other hand, drugs such as heroin and cocaine that have no accepted medical value, or drugs that are very harmful or addictive, are usually illegal. MDMA is an illegal drug with no accepted medical use.

Some drugs come from natural sources, such as plants or mushrooms, while others are created artificially with chemicals. MDMA is a synthetic (human-made) drug created in laboratories.

Drugs are divided into different categories according to their effects and chemical makeup. For example, alcohol is a depressant, or "downer," because it slows down the normal activity of the body when consumed. Caffeine, on the other hand, is a stimulant, or "upper," because it speeds up the body's activities. Drugs that affect the mind or behavior are known as psychoactive drugs. Some psychoactive drugs cause users to see images or hear sounds that don't really exist. This sensory experience is called a hallucination. A drug that causes hallucinations is called a hallucinogen.

Ecstasy is a psychoactive drug. It is classified as a hallucinogen because it can cause distortions in how you see things. It also acts like a group of stimulants called amphetamines. Like amphetamines, ecstasy speeds up the body's activities.

Drugs also differ in the way they are taken and how much they cost. In the case of ecstasy, it is often taken orally (through the mouth), but it can also be snorted (inhaled through the nose), taken intravenously (injected through a vein directly into the bloodstream), or smoked. The drug comes in the form of a tablet, capsule, or loose powder. Each hit of ecstasy generally costs between $10 and $30.

Use of ecstasy has been on the decline since 2001. According to the 2009 Monitoring the Future survey, 6.5 percent of twelfth graders, 5.5 percent of tenth graders, and 2.2 percent of eighth graders had used ecstasy at least once. Though use with teens has been declining, overall use by Americans has increased. According to the 2008 National Survey on Drug Use and Health, there were 615,000 first-time users in 2005, whereas that number climbed to 894,000 first-time users in 2008.

But just because teen use is down, it's no reason not to be informed. When people aren't informed about drug use, they can take for granted the risks involved. Most young people get information about ecstasy by word of mouth in places such as raves, for example. In this way, they learn where to buy it, what its effects are, and whether it can hurt them.

All kinds of rumors have spread about ecstasy. Some people claim that ecstasy taps your spinal fluid and can permanently

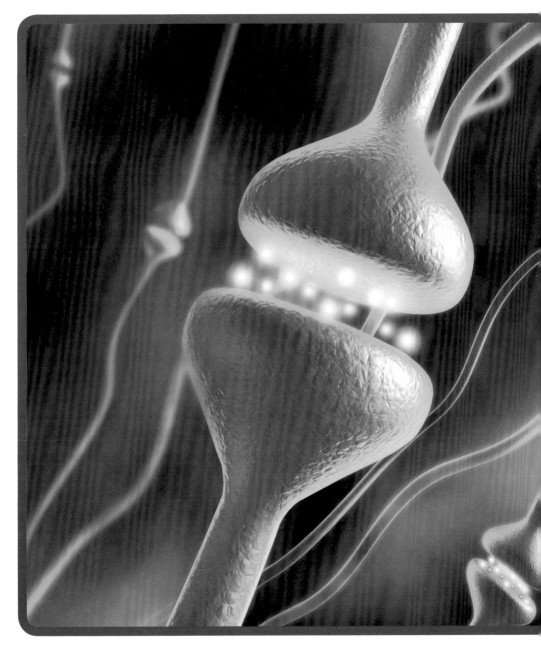

The use of ecstasy causes your brain to increase the release of serotonin, which is passed by your nerve cells through your body.

paralyze you. Others say that ecstasy has no negative side effects. Both of these rumors are false. The rest of this chapter will sort out the facts from the myths about the effects of ecstasy.

What X Does Once It Is Inside Your Body

Ecstasy affects the body's central nervous system: the brain and the spinal cord. Once swallowed, ecstasy enters the bloodstream and is carried throughout the body. Some reaches the brain, and some is broken down by the liver. Once inside the brain, ecstasy increases the circulation of a substance called serotonin.

Serotonin is one of several substances in the brain that regulates your mood and how you feel. It is believed to trigger feelings of love and excitement. The high that ecstasy produces is the result of the brain being flooded with "feel-good" serotonin. Ecstasy forces the brain to change moods and maintain the high feeling for about four hours. During this time, ecstasy prevents the brain from calming down by blocking the return and storage of serotonin. Normally, serotonin is released for immediate use and then stored for future use.

When the brain is drained of serotonin, the good feeling fades and users "crash." They feel tired, depressed, and unable to focus. These symptoms can last for hours, days, and sometimes even weeks.

MYTHS & FACTS

MYTH There are no long-term side effects from using ecstasy.

FACT The use of ecstasy can lead to serious long-term loss of brain function, memory impairment, depression, and anxiety. These effects can happen after long periods of use or even after the first use because you can never know for sure what has been added to the pill.

MYTH Each pill has the same effect.

FACT Because its manufacture is not regulated, ecstasy pills can contain other drugs, many of which are harmful, and can vary greatly in strength.

MYTH Ecstasy is not addictive.

FACT Users of the drug experience a psychological dependence. Every drug that interferes with neurotransmitter activity, as ecstasy does with serotonin, causes physiological changes in the brain that can lead to a rebound effect, tolerance, and craving that are hallmarks of physical addiction.

Outside Factors Affect the Experience

Ecstasy is a psychoactive drug. Psychoactive drugs usually make the user's mood or feelings more intense. A user's

Ecstasy is often taken in party settings. The atmosphere where ecstasy is taken and the mind-set of the person taking it are both majors factors in how the drug will affect the user.

mood may depend on the "set and setting" of the drug experience.

The "set" refers to your mind-set or what you are feeling and thinking at the time of your drug experience. If you are

nervous and worried before taking ecstasy, you will probably feel anxious while you're on it. The "setting" is where you are and whom you are with. Taking ecstasy with close friends at home will likely produce a different experience than taking it at a crowded dance party.

How Does It Feel?

Users typically begin to feel the effects of a moderate dose of ecstasy (75–100 milligrams) twenty to sixty minutes after swallowing it. The high lasts about four hours.

Some users experience unpleasant physical symptoms, which may include dryness of the mouth, jaw clenching, faintness, chills, sweating, muscle tension, nausea or vomiting, dilated pupils, and blurred vision. Ecstasy also increases the heart rate, blood pressure, and body temperature.

PERSONAL STORY

Channon took her friend Lisa to her first rave. "You're really going to love this party," Channon told Lisa. "I can't believe you've never been to one before."

At the party Lisa was very self-conscious and felt geeky when she saw the other girls dressed up, dancing, and laughing confidently. Then a guy with bleached blonde hair and a nose ring approached her. Lisa thought he was cute. The guy introduced himself as Cody, and Lisa told him her name.

"Listen, Lisa, do you want to have a good time tonight?" Cody asked. Lisa said, "Yeah." Cody led her to a corner of the room. From his pocket he produced a few small white pills. "It's a small pill, but it's full of fun," he said, laughing.

How could she resist him? Lisa thought to herself that being with Cody might help her have a good time. Still, she hesitated. When Cody said that it was harmless, Lisa slowly took one of the white pills and quickly swallowed it. An hour passed, and Lisa and Cody were dancing together. I feel so alive, Lisa thought. The music was blaring loud. Cody just smiled and put his arms around her.

Two months later Lisa and Cody were still hanging out. Both were taking ecstasy and cutting school regularly. They got high and spent time hanging around the mall. When Lisa was not with Cody and not taking ecstasy, she would sometimes feel so low that it was too much for her even to get out of bed.

MDMA takes its popular street name from the word "ecstasy"—a state of intense emotion. That is because users experience an initial rush of euphoria and become very energetic and confident. This rush is followed by calmness and an absence of worry or anger. These feelings generally last two to three hours. Some users say that ecstasy makes them more expressive and outgoing. They may talk and smile a lot or want to hug the people around them.

Ecstasy also changes the way you perceive things. Users often report heightened senses of touch, hearing, vision, taste, and smell. For example, simple actions, like running your fingers through your hair, may feel intensely pleasurable and new. Colors and sounds may seem clearer or more vivid.

Raves—with their nonstop music, light and video shows, and hundreds of dancers—lend themselves to the ecstasy experience because they indulge the senses and satisfy a user's desire to feel close to others.

CHAPTER 2

THE HISTORY OF ECSTASY

Although MDMA was developed more than eighty years ago, it was not widely used as a recreational drug until the 1980s.

A chemical company called Merck first made MDMA in Germany in 1912. It was created as a diet pill, but there is no evidence that suggests that it was ever used or sold for this purpose.

In 1965, MDMA was re-created in the United States by a chemist named Alexander Shulgin. He shared his discovery with a small group of friends, including some psychiatrists.

During the 1970s, small groups of psychiatrists began experimenting with MDMA as an aid in psychotherapy (treatment of mental disorders). They believed that patients who took MDMA in a relaxed setting under a doctor's supervision could benefit from the drug by releasing their fears, enabling them to communicate freely. With the help of MDMA, patients could work through many of their problems. The doctors compared the drug's effects to Adam's innocent and blissful state in the biblical Garden of Eden, before he ate the forbidden fruit from the Tree of Knowledge. For this reason, they called the drug "Adam."

In the early 1980s, some small drug manufacturers learned of the euphoric feelings caused by MDMA and started producing the drug for recreational use. Some bars in Dallas and Fort Worth, Texas, began selling ecstasy to young professionals and young adults and promoting "ecstasy parties." The hype over ecstasy began to spread, and the demand and supply for the drug grew rapidly across the nation. At the time, MDMA was not yet categorized as a controlled substance under federal law and was, therefore, still legal.

The Controlled Substances Act of 1970 places all substances that are regulated by federal law into one of five schedules, or categories. Substances are classified according to their safety, medical uses, and potential for abuse. All drugs within the same schedule are subject to the same legal restrictions and penalties.

In June 1985, the Drug Enforcement Administration (DEA) banned MDMA and placed it in the most restrictive category

The American chemist Alexander Shulgin, shown here, was the first to re-create MDMA in the United States. The drug was first made by German chemists in 1912.

of illegal drugs. This category, referred to as Schedule I, also includes heroin and LSD. Schedule I drugs are considered to have a high potential for abuse and no accepted medical use. It is illegal to make, possess, or sell any Schedule I drug in the United States.

The DEA reportedly classified MDMA as a Schedule I drug because researchers found that a chemically related drug, MDA, caused brain damage in rats. This led researchers to question whether MDA and related drugs like MDMA can cause damage in the human brain.

The Rise of Rave Culture

Since the mid-1980s, ecstasy has had a wide appeal among young people who are part of the rave culture. However, its use is not limited to this subculture— people from all walks of life have tried ecstasy.

Raves are makeshift and often illegal parties that take place in abandoned warehouses, parks, or nightclubs. They can last all night long. Raves are popular among teenagers and college students. They can be very large, with thousands of people in attendance.

HERBAL ECSTASY

Since ecstasy became a popular recreational drug, some companies began marketing herbal look-alikes to teens. With attractive packaging and promises of "a floaty, mind-expanding euphoria," products like Herbal Ecstasy have drawn teens who want to experience a legal and natural high.

Herbal Ecstasy was created as a natural alternative to an illegal drug. It should not, however, be mistaken for MDMA. Herbal Ecstasy is not made with the same ingredients as MDMA, nor does it produce the same high. Its main ingredient, ephedra, is a natural stimulant. It raises your blood pressure and heart rate and makes your skin tingle, but it doesn't affect your brain chemistry in the same way that MDMA does.

It is important to bear in mind that natural and legal do not necessarily mean safe. In large doses, herbal alternatives to ecstasy can cause severe side effects. Ephedra has been linked to heart attacks, seizures, and death. The Food and Drug Administration (FDA) has issued a health warning about ephedra, and several states have declared it illegal to sell ephedra products as "mood-altering substances." Ephedra products were once used for weight loss and bodybuilding, but now the FDA is warning people that these uses can be dangerous to your health.

Many raves are illegal because they are unlicensed. To be considered legal, a dance club must follow strict regulations and obtain various permits and licenses.

Unlicensed raves can be very unsafe. Often, too many people are crammed into a space that is not designed to hold so many bodies. There have been cases of unlicensed raves where the floors have caved in beneath the weight of hundreds of dancers. Fire safety regulations are also frequently ignored.

Ecstasy is often taken at late-night dance parties that feature techno, trance, or house music. Some of these parties are illegal because they are not licensed, so they can be dangerous to attend.

Those who organize raves constantly change locations to avoid being shut down. Details about where the next rave will be held usually spread by word of mouth or on social networks. Large parties are also promoted through colorful flyers found at record stores, trendy clothing stores, and skate shops. Many raves have been held at legal nightclubs that offer special rave nights.

At raves, DJs spin techno, trance, and house music to get people dancing. While each kind of music has a distinct sound, all share a hypnotic rhythm, synthesizer sounds, and a general use of samples. Samples are fragments of other people's recordings that are mixed into a new recording through the use of electronic equipment. In this atmosphere, filled with the throbbing intensity of techno music, ravers often turn to drugs like ecstasy to get high and dance all night.

While Americans were using ecstasy even before the rave culture developed in the United States, it is clear that the drug's popularity increased as raves spread across the country. Ecstasy and electronic music inspired the rave dance culture. Together, the drug and the music help create a trancelike state for ravers. Ecstasy became an important part of the rave dance culture in much the same way that LSD became associated with a lot of the psychedelic music of the 1960s, and speed became associated with punk rock. However, it's important to remember that many of the people who go to raves do not take drugs. They get a natural high from dancing to good music and socializing with friends.

PERSONAL STORY

On Saturday night, Logan brought his friend Brianna to a rave. They met their friends Evan and Lila at the party, and all of them were dancing and having a good time.

"This is a blast!" Brianna said. "I can't believe I've been missing out on these parties."

"Here's something else you've been missing out on," Logan said, holding out a small pill to Brianna. "Try it. It's ecstasy. If you think that you feel good now, just wait! You'll feel as though you can do anything once you take it."

Brianna thought about it for a moment. Logan saw her hesitate and said, "C'mon, Bri, I really want to share this with you. It's amazing." Brianna trusted Logan, so she popped the pill into her mouth and waited to feel as great as Logan said she would. It took about thirty minutes before a wave of energy hit Brianna full force. When she danced, Brianna was a bundle of different sensations. All of her insecurities seemed to disappear. She felt totally in sync with the music.

Then things began to change. Brianna felt hot and dehydrated. She was afraid that she might pass out. Brianna looked for Logan, but the lights confused her, and the pounding music made her brain feel as if it would explode. She thought that everyone was looking at her.

Brianna found her friend Evan. "Help me!" she pleaded to him. "I don't feel good."

"Just dance a little more," assured Evan. "It's too early to go home." He was too high on ecstasy to notice how upset Brianna was.

"No! I have to go home! Where is Logan?" Brianna cried. She found Logan a few feet away. "I'm sick," she told him. "I want to go home now!"

"Man, I'm sorry," Logan said. "I didn't mean to get you so messed up." Feeling guilty, he helped Brianna out of the party and waited until a sober friend could come pick her up. Once Brianna felt better, she had some time to think. She was upset with Logan for giving her ecstasy, but she was also angry with herself for taking a drug that was dangerous. Brianna knew that ecstasy would not become a part of her life again.

Not all ecstasy use happens at raves and nightclubs. Some people take ecstasy with friends at someone's house or at smaller parties. Taking ecstasy in a quieter, familiar setting may make you feel safer, but the effects of the drug don't change. You still run the risk of suffering serious consequences.

A well-known ecstasy-related tragedy that really resonated with people around the world occurred in 1995. A British teenager named Leah Betts fell into a coma after taking ecstasy at her eighteenth birthday party while her parents were home. She reportedly drank too much water to make up for the dehydrating effects of ecstasy. Her body was unable to eliminate enough water through sweating or urinating. She died when her body filled up with excess fluid.

Ignorance Isn't Bliss

MDMA, or ecstasy, is an illegal substance made in underground (secret) laboratories. This means that you can never be certain about its purity or dosage because you don't know who made it, what was put into it, or how much of the drug was used. Compare this to a legal drug like cold medicine, where you know the company that made a certain product, its ingredients, and potential side effects. Producers of legal drugs must meet strict government quality standards to ensure that their products are pure. On the other hand, those who make illegal drugs like MDMA are not subject to such controls.

These ecstasy tablets are made to look like children's vitamins. Not only can the appearance of ecstasy pills change, so can what is in them, which affects how dangerous they are.

As a result, much of the ecstasy sold on the street is not pure MDMA. It is often "cut," or mixed, with contaminants (other substances) by the dealers who sell it in order to increase their profits. Contaminants may include cold medicine ingredients, harmless fillers, or even poisons. Other illegal drugs, like speed, heroin, or LSD, are sometimes found in ecstasy tablets. These substances may produce undesired or unexpected effects that can seriously harm you.

CHAPTER 3

THE RISKS OF ROLLING

Ecstasy is not a risk-free drug. While it can give the user an intense high, it can also cause dangerous side effects and "bad trips."

Not all teens feel good after taking ecstasy. Some feel very anxious, confused, or paranoid while on the drug. They may even have a panic attack—a feeling of overwhelming fear with symptoms, such as nausea, hyperventilation, sweating, and rapid heartbeat. Such attacks can be dangerous because

Some teens who take ecstasy react with feelings of anxiousness, confusion, and paranoia. They may also feel depressed for days or even weeks after the high wears off.

people rarely think clearly or use good judgment when they are so scared. Teens who are angry or upset before using ecstasy may become moody or violent when they are high because ecstasy tends to exaggerate the user's mood.

Ecstasy can trick your mind into seeing objects differently than they appear. You may "see" trails of blurred images or objects vibrating when the objects are, in fact, still. This distortion can affect your judgment and coordination and lead to serious injury. For example, a person who is dancing on a stage while on ecstasy may become so wrapped up in the flashing of the surrounding lights that he or she may fall off the stage.

Ecstasy increases your chances of worsening an injury because it decreases your sensitivity to pain. You might hurt yourself while you're high and not even know it until the effects of the drug wear off.

When users come down from an ecstasy high, they often experience body chills. Some people have trouble walking after taking large doses of ecstasy; they feel like they can't move their legs. Hours later, they may suffer pain in their lower back, joints, and muscles. Some people become irritable when coming off of ecstasy. Many have trouble falling asleep.

They may feel very tired the next day and eat very little. It is not unusual to feel listless and depressed for days.

Some people feel the side effects of ecstasy even weeks after use. They may suffer from depression, anxiety, and even paranoia. Those who already suffer from depression may have

DRUG COCKTAILS: THE DANGERS OF MIXING SUBSTANCES

A further danger involved in using ecstasy is not knowing exactly what you are taking or how strong it is. Ecstasy is frequently mixed with other drugs or substances that can cause unpredictable reactions. For example, taking ecstasy that is laced with LSD may cause you to hallucinate for up to twelve hours. This "trip" can be very scary and dangerous if you are not expecting it.

You also don't know how strong an ecstasy pill will be. Very high doses of ecstasy cause the user to be more alert and excited than euphoric. This may result in a dissatisfying or dangerous high.

The only way to be sure of what is in an ecstasy pill is to have it tested. Some nightclubs in the Netherlands have ecstasy testing booths that analyze tablets for contaminants. In the United States, such testing is not available. The bottom line is that you never know what you are getting when you take ecstasy.

Some young people who experiment with ecstasy intentionally mix different drugs to get higher during their trip or to come down easier. This can be very dangerous for many reasons. For example, mixing ecstasy with an amphetamine—a drug often used by ravers to feel more energetic—greatly increases your risk of overheating, particularly in a crowded party setting where you are likely to lose fluids by sweating. Drinking alcohol when you are high on ecstasy is dangerous because both drugs cause dehydration and put a lot of stress on your liver. People who take antidepressants should also avoid taking ecstasy because the combination can cause dangerously high blood pressure.

long-term anxiety disorders that make them feel nervous all the time.

In rare cases, frequent users have suffered long-term consequences, including liver and kidney damage and psychosis—a mental condition in which a person loses touch with reality.

Complications and Casualties Resulting from Ecstasy

Little is known about ecstasy's long-term effects on the human body and mind. This is partly because it has only recently become popular as a recreational drug. And since it is an illegal drug, the government has allowed limited research on the effects of MDMA in humans. According to the National Institute on Drug Abuse (NIDA), studies on nonhuman primates that had exposure to MDMA for four days revealed damage to serotonin nerve terminals that had still not healed six and seven years later. Though this evidence has not yet been proved in humans, such government-approved studies are the continuing focus of researchers in determining whether MDMA causes brain damage and other long-term health hazards. What is known is that young people have suffered complications after taking ecstasy, and some have died.

Overdosing on ecstasy, or taking too much of the drug for your body to handle, can cause you to vomit continuously, hyperventilate, or pass out. If you have a pre-existing health condition, such as heart, liver, or kidney problems, or if you

Ecstasy has a tendency to hide your sense of thirst. A person on ecstasy who is losing a lot of fluids from dancing and sweating may not notice that he or she is becoming dehydrated and needs to drink water.

suffer from asthma, epilepsy, diabetes, or depression, taking ecstasy is a particularly serious health risk. But even young people in good health have suffered permanent damage after taking ecstasy.

One of the most common reasons for complications or death associated with ecstasy use is overheating or heatstroke. Heatstroke occurs when the body's internal thermometer fails, and the body is exposed to excessive heat. Your body is usually able to maintain a stable internal temperature even when it is very hot outside. If your body temperature rises, your body sweats to cool off. But when you are exposed to high temperatures for a long time, your body may not be able to cool off sufficiently. In extreme cases, heatstroke can lead to seizure, coma, or death.

Several incidents of heatstroke have been linked to ecstasy use at raves. Research suggests that ecstasy itself increases body temperature and can cause dehydration. The stimulant effect of ecstasy can also contribute, indirectly, to causing heatstroke. That is because ecstasy enables users to dance longer than they normally would without feeling tired. They often dance for hours in a hot and crowded area without taking a break to cool down or replenish the fluids they've lost from sweating.

Ecstasy tends to hide your sense of thirst even when your body is being drained of fluids as you sweat. Since ecstasy can mask the danger signals of overheating, victims may not even try to cool down or drink when they are hot and dehydrated.

Danger signs of heatstroke include an abnormally high body temperature (about 105° F/40.5° C), rapid heartbeat, quick and shallow breathing, and abnormally high or low blood pressure. Faintness, confusion, and panic attacks can also occur.

If you detect a danger sign of heatstroke, you should retreat immediately to an area that is quiet and cool. Sit or lay down. Rest and drink fluids like water or fruit juice. Let friends or someone you can trust know about your condition so that they can seek emergency medical help, if necessary. You should

PERSONAL STORY

The last time Bailey's brother Robby was home from college, she took ecstasy with him. "Can you bring me some more of that when you come home next weekend?" Bailey asked him.

Bailey saved the small bag of pills from Robby for a weekend when her parents were out of town. She invited her cousin Peter, her friend Cassie, and Peter's best friend, Jake, over for an evening of fun involving ecstasy. Cassie was a little nervous about taking the drug, but the others were doing it, and Bailey assured her that she loved the feeling it gave her. Cassie was still unsure, but she didn't want to feel left out.

They all swallowed the brown-speckled pills and waited for the drug to take effect. But when it finally did take effect, it wasn't as Bailey had promised. First Cassie began to vomit uncontrollably. Then Peter said that he thought he was going to pass out. Jake threw up and then passed out. Bailey became extremely drowsy, but she was able to call her brother at school for help.

When Robby arrived at the house, he found the group desperately ill. He called 911, and an ambulance rushed them to the hospital. Luckily, all of them felt better in the morning after being treated.

The next day, Robby checked with the guy who supplied him with the supposed ecstasy pills. It turned out that the pills he gave to Bailey probably contained heroin. Robby felt awful about what had happened to his sister and her friend, and he knew it could have been worse. He had no idea that ecstasy could be laced with another drug.

be treated with cool compresses and fanned as you wait for help to arrive.

In some cases, death has resulted from drinking too much water. Drinking more fluids than your body can get rid of can cause kidney failure and other complications. Drinking lots of water and not urinating is a dangerous sign that your body is not functioning properly. Seek emergency medical help if you detect this danger sign.

Risky Behavior

Teens who use ecstasy think they are on top of the world and can do anything. This attitude can lead to unreasonable and dangerous behavior. For example, you may want to drive your car even though you are high. This kind of poor judgment can get you into a serious accident and put the lives of innocent people at risk.

Ecstasy tends to make people feel more emotional and sensual. Some users express affection toward strangers, which may be misinterpreted and taken advantage of. Users may become more open to physical intimacy than they normally would be. They may make decisions that they might regret. It's easy to forget about protected sex when you're high. But it won't be so easy to forget about an unwanted pregnancy or a sexually transmitted disease (STD) if you catch one. It only takes one unprotected sexual encounter to get pregnant or contract HIV, the virus that causes the incurable disease AIDS.

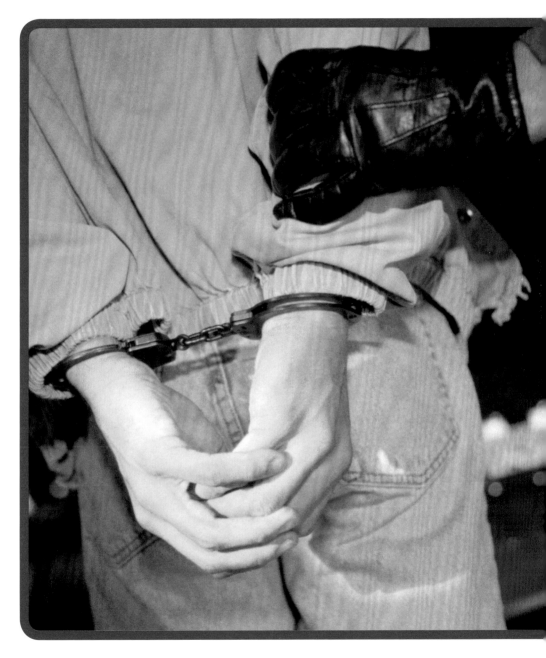

Driving while under the influence of ecstasy—or any drug—is extremely dangerous. It can also get you arrested, put on probation, or even sent to a juvenile detention center.

Legal Troubles

Getting involved with ecstasy can get you into trouble with the law. Driving under the influence (DUI) or driving while intoxicated (DWI) and possessing or selling an illegal drug can send you straight to jail. If you are a minor and are caught with ecstasy, you will likely be sent to a juvenile detention center and may be sentenced to a one-year probation. If you are over eighteen years old, you may be sent to prison for up to five years.

Ecstasy is an expensive drug. Most teens cannot afford to use it regularly. Some teens have resorted to stealing from family and friends or robbing strangers to get money to buy ecstasy. Frequent users sometimes buy ecstasy in quantities of ten hits or more. They then resell it at a higher price to cover the costs of their own doses. Whether you buy ten hits to share with your friends or to sell to strangers, you are considered a drug dealer in the eyes of the law and will be prosecuted accordingly.

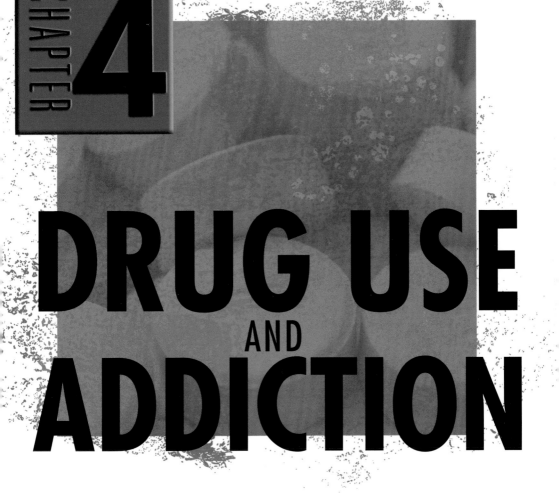

CHAPTER 4

DRUG USE AND ADDICTION

Being a teen means changing, trying new things, and deciding what you like to do. This is the time that you begin to develop your identity. You want to act like an adult and make your own decisions. Some teens experiment with drugs during this time of change to feel independent and explore new feelings.

Most teens who try drugs for the first time are curious. They want to know what will happen, how they will feel, or

The teen years are a difficult and transitional time. However, using drugs like ecstasy to fit in with peers or to forget anxieties only creates more problems.

what they will see. Curiosity is a natural feeling. It is very dangerous, though, to use a drug just because you are curious.

Some teens turn to drugs to cope with the pressures of adolescence. For example, it is common in school to want to fit in and do what everyone else is doing. Others around you may be experimenting with drugs. This may seem like an easy way to look cool or feel like part of the "in" crowd.

As a teenager, you may feel very insecure, especially about the way you look because your body is changing so much. You may take drugs to forget your anxieties and feel more confident. Drugs are often used as a way to cope with, or block out, problems. Some teens have trouble at home or at school and feel like they have no one to turn to for help. They may take drugs to feel better. After the high wears off, though, they often feel worse than they did before. Taking drugs doesn't make your problems disappear; it only creates more problems.

Some teens think that drug use is acceptable because they see their parents or siblings abusing drugs. The media—magazines, television, and movies—which sometimes glamorize drugs, may also influence the public's attitude toward drugs. Seeing a favorite actor using drugs in a movie may lead you to think that drugs are OK.

Teens turn to drugs like ecstasy for many different reasons: to feel happy, to feel more secure in social settings, or to forget their problems. Yet ecstasy and other drugs only offer a temporary and artificial sense of control, confidence, and happiness. Lasting happiness can't come from a drug.

Understanding Addiction

When a drug user feels an intense desire to use a drug that is known to be harmful and continues to give into the craving, he or she may become addicted. If the user satisfies this craving frequently, he or she can quickly build up a tolerance to the

SELF-ASSESSMENT

How are drugs affecting your life? If you think you or a friend may have a drug problem, take the following self-test for teens from the National Council on Alcoholism and Drug Dependence:

- Do you use drugs to build self-confidence?
- Do you ever drink or get high immediately after you have a problem at home or at school?
- Have you ever missed school due to drugs?
- Does it bother you if someone says that you use too much alcohol or other drugs?
- Have you started hanging out with a heavy-drinking or drug-using crowd?
- Are drugs affecting your reputation?
- Do you borrow money or "do without" other things to buy drugs?
- Do you feel guilty after using drugs?
- Do you feel a sense of power when you use drugs?
- Do you use drugs until your supply is gone?
- Have you lost friends since you started using drugs?
- Do you feel more at ease in social situations when using drugs?
- Have you ever been arrested or hospitalized due to use of alcohol or illegal drugs?
- Has anyone in your family had drinking or other drug problems?
- Do you ever wake up and wonder what happened the night before?

If you answered "yes" to several of these questions, you may have a drug problem. The following chapter provides information on ways to get help.

drug, needing more each time to achieve the same effect. This occurs because the body becomes less responsive to the effects of a drug after repeated use. A user may feel the need to use a drug even if it no longer produces any sense of pleasure. An addict sometimes suffers painful physical and psychological symptoms, or withdrawal symptoms, that occur when he or she stops taking the drug.

The levels of addiction differ from drug to drug. Some drugs, like heroin and alcohol, are physically addictive. This means that an addict's body needs the drug on a regular basis; otherwise, he or she will suffer withdrawal symptoms, such as nausea or stomach cramps.

Other drugs, like ecstasy, can be psychologically addictive. This means that users feel the need to use a drug to feel good, but they won't necessarily suffer physical withdrawal symptoms without it. They may, however, suffer psychological withdrawal symptoms, such as severe depression and anxiety. Psychological dependence on a drug may be subtler than physical addiction, but it isn't any less serious.

Generally, a person's first experience with ecstasy is the strongest. Continued use over a long period of time brings diminishing returns, or fewer positive and more negative effects. Tolerance develops to ecstasy's euphoric effects, and the drug begins to feel more like a "speed rush." Because the user doesn't feel the same high over time, ecstasy is less likely to be abused for very long periods than most other "hard" drugs.

Some drug dealers will give free ecstasy to first-time users. Their hope is that these first-timers will become hooked on the euphoric feeling and become repeat customers.

How Do You Get Hooked?

The road to drug addiction usually starts with experimental use, when teens first try drugs. Most start experimenting with alcohol, cigarettes, or marijuana. If they like the experience, they may eventually move on to harder drugs to get a more intense high. Repeated use of a habit-forming drug can easily develop into addiction.

Some users get trapped in a cycle of drug dependency by becoming part of a social scene that involves drugs. For example, teens who go to raves often experiment with ecstasy because drugs are part of the scene. Sometimes, dealers give free ecstasy to first-time users to hook them on the drug. Some teens feel great the first time they use ecstasy, so they try it again. Many find that their high isn't quite the same the second time, so they try ecstasy over and over again in an attempt to recapture their first experience with the drug.

Binge users take from three to ten hits of ecstasy at a time. Often, they "boost" or "stack" their dosage by taking more hits throughout the trip to lengthen their high. However, taking multiple or repeated doses of ecstasy usually increases the stimulant effect, not the euphoria. By not allowing the body to go through its normal mood cycles, the user will eventually crash and feel so depressed that he or she will want to do more of the drug.

PERSONAL STORY

Brandon has been acting weird lately. His best friend, Hunter, was the first to notice. It started when Brandon went to a rave a few months ago. Since then he's been hitting the scene every single weekend. Hunter knows that Brandon takes a lot of ecstasy at these parties, and it worries him.

One day, Brandon asked Hunter if he could copy his homework, since he had been out late the night before. Hunter didn't know whether it would help Brandon to let him copy his homework or not. He told Brandon that he wasn't going to help him cheat. Brandon got mad and shoved him so hard that it nearly knocked Hunter off his feet. He then started hitting and punching Hunter, until Hunter finally yelled out, "Stop it, Brandon! What's wrong with you?"

Brandon stopped what he was doing and looked at Hunter. He had a look of shock on his face. "I'm sorry," he said. "Ecstasy is controlling my life." Brandon felt bad about what he had done to Hunter. He was not only hurting himself, but he was also hurting his friend.

Hunter put his arm around Brandon's shoulder to comfort him. "Come on, let's get you to the guidance counselor for some help," he said.

How Drugs Take Over

Depression is one of the side effects of ecstasy use, and users often depend on ecstasy to bring them out of their depression. But many users find that the more they use ecstasy, the more they become depressed when they are not high. Although they feel miserable much of the time, they can't bring themselves to

Prolonged use of ecstasy can sometimes lead to depression. Users who become depressed often continue to use ecstasy to feel better, but this only worsens the condition.

stop using ecstasy because it brings temporary relief to their depression. They become caught in a no-win situation.

Drug addiction dominates your life. It takes your attention away from important social activities, including school, work, and spending time with family and friends. If you are addicted to a drug, you will continue to use it even if you hurt yourself or those around you. Repeated use of ecstasy can wreak havoc on your health, social life, mental ability, and sense of well-being.

5

GETTING HELP

I f you have a serious drug addiction, you need to get professional help. You are only hurting yourself in the long run if you don't. Admitting that you have a problem is a major step toward becoming well. There are people and places that can help you out.

Dialing for Help

If you think that you have a drug problem, one of the easiest ways to get help is to call a drug hotline set up by organizations

The first step to kicking an ecstasy—or other drug—habit is to admit that you have a problem and seek help. Trained drug counselors are always available to help.

for people who are ready to kick their drug habit. Remember, they are there to help and won't judge you. When you call, you'll speak with a trained counselor. You may want to start out by asking the counselor a few general questions, such as, "How do I know if I have a drug problem?" until you feel comfortable talking to this person. The counselor is trained to listen to you,

TEN GREAT QUESTIONS TO ASK A DOCTOR

1. How do I know if I have a drug problem?

2. How does drug treatment work?

3. Is drug treatment effective?

4. How will I feel when I stop taking drugs?

5. How long will it take me to quit drugs?

6. How will it change me?

7. What will happen to me if I use drugs again?

8. How do I tell my parents and friends that I am getting treatment for drug use?

9. Some of my friends use, too; how can I help them get help?

10. Will my recovery take place at home, or will I have to go away?

answer your questions, and offer you advice on how to take care of your problem. You don't even have to tell the counselor your name. This person will not get you in trouble with your parents. The counselor will never judge you, nor will he or she report you to the authorities.

Counseling

You would probably benefit from some face-to-face counseling as well. If you cannot talk to your parents, you can talk to other people such as an older friend or relative, your favorite teacher, or your school counselor. They can help you get in touch with a local drug treatment clinic where you can talk to a counselor either for free or at a low cost.

Getting help for drug abuse can involve talking to a parent or an older friend or relative whom you trust. You can also ask a teacher or school counselor for advice.

When you enter a clinic, you will meet with a counselor one-on-one. It is important to talk to your counselor about your problems because he or she is there to listen and help you. Your counselor may ask you questions about why you

Joining a support group is a great way to help you overcome drug abuse and addiction. You will be able to talk to other users who may have the same fears and concerns as you do.

think you need drugs and what benefit you think they have on your life. He or she may explain how you went from just experimenting with drugs to being addicted to them. This is all part of the drug education you will receive.

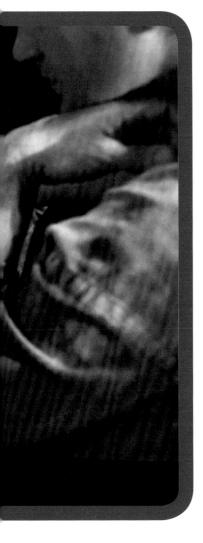

You Can't Do It Alone

You will be encouraged to join a support group in which you share your drug experiences with other drug users like yourself. You may feel nervous and shy at first about sharing your story openly with strangers. However, you may find it helpful to listen to the stories of other teens who have experienced some of the same things that you have. Once you accept your mistakes and commit yourself to getting your life straightened out, you are on the road to recovery. You are not alone. Others are going through the very same thing. You have the support you need to turn your life around.

If your drug problem is seriously out of control, you may need inpatient treatment. Inpatient treatment

PERSONAL STORY

At the drug counselor's office, Brandon was given two choices. He could continue to use drugs and probably ruin his chances at having a normal life. Or he could stop using drugs, stay in school, and pursue his dream of becoming an app and software developer. Brandon was already tiring of the same old routine of getting high, crashing when the ecstasy wore off, and then getting high again. He was beginning to feel as though his life wasn't going anywhere.

Brandon's school counselor referred him to a local outreach center. Brandon was nervous, so Hunter went with him. The counselor at the center was very understanding and made Brandon feel comfortable. She didn't make him feel guilty for doing drugs, and she encouraged him to join the center's support group for teen drug users. As part of the support group, Brandon spoke about his addiction.

Gradually he made new friends and began rebuilding his life. Brandon is now back at school after a brief stay at a drug rehabilitation clinic. He is taking computer classes and maintains his own Web site. His family, friends, and teachers are proud of his accomplishments. Everyone seems impressed with his talent and drive. They know how hard it was for him to get over his addiction to ecstasy. Brandon's dedication to ending his addiction got him to where he is now—recovery. He knows that a drug-free existence is the key to reaching his goals and having the life he wants.

means that you live at the clinic or hospital for full-time help. This is never easy, but your recovery is well worth the struggle ahead.

You may realize that you do not need drugs to feel good about yourself and have a good time. In fact, drugs end up doing the opposite. They prevent you from paying attention in school and learning all you need to know to get ahead in the world. Spending time in pursuit of your dreams is a much better way to achieve a personal high than doing drugs. The choice is yours.

GLOSSARY

addiction A condition in which a person craves a drug intensely and is unable to stop using it despite the harm it causes.

amphetamine A stimulant drug that speeds up the processes of the body.

anxiety Fear, worry, or dread.

contaminant An impurity or filler added to a pure substance.

dehydration The loss of body fluids or water.

depression A state of sadness marked by feelings of hopelessness and withdrawal from daily activities.

diminishing returns A decrease in the pleasurable effects of a drug caused by tolerance developed through regular use.

drug A nonfood substance that affects your mind and body.

ecstasy A state of sudden and intense emotion; also the name of a drug that produces strong joyous feelings.

euphoria A feeling of happiness and well-being.

hallucination A sensory experience in which a person sees or hears things that do not really exist.

hallucinogen A substance that causes hallucinations.

heatstroke A condition in which the body's thermometer breaks down, and the body is overexposed to heat.

hyperventilate To breathe abnormally, rapidly, and deeply.

overdose An excessive amount of a drug that can cause severe damage or death.

panic attack A collection of negative, frightening thoughts and feelings that becomes out of control.

psychoactive Describing a drug that affects one's mood and behavior.

rave A large dance party with techno music and light and video shows.

serotonin A brain chemical that is believed to regulate one's mood.

synthetic Made from a chemical process; not made naturally.

techno music A style of dance music heard at raves and nightclubs. It consists of fast rhythms and sampled synthesizer music.

tolerance The resistance to a drug's effects gained through continuous use.

withdrawal symptom A painful physical or psychological symptom that occurs when a person stops using an addictive drug.

FOR MORE INFORMATION

Canadian Centre on Substance Abuse
75 Albert Street, Suite 500
Ottawa, ON K1P 5E7
Canada
(613) 235-4048
Web site: http://www.ccsa.ca
The Canadian Centre on Substance Abuse strives
to lead the nation in efforts to reduce harm
to society caused by drugs and alcohol.

Centre for Addictions Research of BC (CARBC)
University of Victoria
Technology Enterprise Facility
2300 McKenzie Avenue, Room 273
Victoria, BC V8P 5C2
Canada
(250) 472-5445
Web site: http://www.carbc.ca
The Centre for Addictions Research of BC is
dedicated to disseminating research findings
and increasing awareness and understanding
of substance use and addiction.

ClubDrugs.gov
6001 Executive Boulevard
Bethesda, MD 20892-9561

(301) 443-1124

Web site: http://www.clubdrugs.gov

ClubDrugs.gov is a service of the National Institute on Drug
Abuse that focuses on the dangers of using club drugs such
as ecstasy, ketamine, and GHB.

DEAL (Delivering Education and Awareness for Life)

C101 – 1200 Vanier Parkway

Ottawa, ON K1A 0R2

Canada

Web site: http://www.deal.org

DEAL is a resource, provided by the Youth Engagement Section
of the Royal Canadian Mounted Police, to help teens in
Canada find information on a number of difficult issues that
they may encounter in life. Maintained by young people,
DEAL hosts a blog, fact sheets, and a list of initiatives hap-
pening in communities across Canada.

Narcotics Anonymous (NA)

P.O. Box 9999

Van Nuys, CA 91409

(818) 773-9999

Web site: http://www.na.org

NA is a support group that follows a twelve-step recovery
model. The group holds regular meetings in communities
across the nation and the world.

Partnership at Drugfree.org
352 Park Avenue South, 9th Floor
New York, NY 10010
(212) 922-1560
Web site: http://www.drugfree.org
Partnership at Drugfree.org is a nonprofit organization that
provides resources to parents across the country to under-
stand and help prevent drug use, and offers tools on how
to step in and help children who may be abusing drugs.

Phoenix House
164 West 74th Street
New York, NY
(800) 378-4435
Web site: http://www.phoenixhouse.org
Phoenix House is the largest nonprofit drug and alcohol treatment and prevention facility in the United States. It has been
providing residential and outreach programs since 1967.

Web Sites

Due to the changing nature of Internet links, Rosen Publishing
has developed an online list of Web sites related to the subject
of this book. This site is updated regularly. Please use this link to
access the list:

http://www.rosenlinks.com/dac/ecs

FOR FURTHER READING

Bankston, John. *Ecstasy = Busted!* Berkley Heights, NJ: Enslow Publishers, 2005.

Connolly, Sean. *Ecstasy*. North Mankato, MN: Smart Apple Media, 2007.

Espejo, Roman, ed. *Club Drugs*. Farmington Hills, MI: Greenhaven Press, 2009.

Fitzguh, Karla. *Ecstasy*. Chicago, IL: Heinemann Library, 2006.

Gordon, Olivia. *The Agony of Ecstasy.* New York, NY: Continuum International Publishing Group, 2006.

Green, Jared F., ed. *DJ, Dance, and Rave Culture*. Farmington Hills, MI: Greenhaven Press, 2005.

Iversen, Leslie. *Speed, Ecstasy, Ritalin: The Science of Amphetamines*. New York, NY: Oxford University Press, 2006.

Karson, Jill. *Club Drugs*. San Diego, CA: ReferencePoint Press, 2008.

Koellhoffer, Tara. *Ecstasy and Other Club Drugs*. New York, NY: Chelsea House, 2008.

Kuhn, Cynthia, Scott Swartzwelder, and Wilkie Wilson. *Buzzed: The Straight Facts About the Most Used and Abused Drugs from Alcohol to Ecstasy*. New York, NY: W. W. Norton, 2008.

Lane, Stephanie. *Ecstasy*. Farmington Hills, MI: Lucent Books, 2006.

Marcovitz, Hal. *Club Drugs*. Farmington Hills, MI: Lucent Books, 2006.

Pilcher, Tim. *E: The Incredibly Strange History of Ecstasy*. Philadelphia, PA: Running Press, 2008.

Olive, M. Foster. *Ecstasy*. New York, NY: Chelsea House, 2009.

Orr, Tamra. *Ecstasy*. New York, NY: Rosen Publishing, 2008.

Swarts, Katherine, ed. *Club Drugs*. Farmington Hills, MI: Greenhaven Press, 2006.

INDEX

A

addiction
  how it happens, 45–47
  self-assesment, 42
  signs of, 13, 39–43
  ten questions to ask a doctor, 50
  treatment, 48–53
alcohol, 31, 43, 45
amphetamines, 10, 31
antidepressants, 31
anxiety, 13, 15, 30, 43

B

brain, 12, 13, 21, 22, 32

C

chills, 30
Controlled Substances Act of 1970, 19–21

D

dehydration/dryness, 15, 25, 26, 31, 34
depressants, 9
depression, 12, 30, 33, 43, 45, 46–47
driving under the influence (DUI), 38
driving while intoxicated (DWI), 38

Drug Enforcement Administration (DEA), 20–21

E

ecstasy (MDMA)
  health risks, 4, 6, 13, 28–36
  how it was developed, 18–21
  illegal behavior, 38
  myths and facts about, 13
  personal stories, 16, 25, 35, 46, 54
  use statistics, 10
  what happens when you take it, 10–12, 14–17
  what it is, 4–6, 9, 10
ephedra, 22

F

fatalities, 4, 6, 22, 26, 32, 34, 36
fatigue, 12, 30

H

hallucinogen, 9, 10
heatstroke, 4, 31, 33–34, 36
Herbal Ecstasy, 22

K

kidneys, 32, 36

L

liver, 12, 31, 32

M

memory impairment, 13
Merck, 18

O

overhydrating, 26, 36

P

pain, decreased sensitivity to, 30
panic attacks, 28–30, 34
paranoia, 30
pregnancy, 36
psychoactive drugs, 9, 10, 14
psychosis, 32

R

raves, 10, 16, 17, 21–26, 34, 45, 46

S

serotonin, 12, 13, 32
"set and setting" and drug use, 15
sexually transmitted diseases (STDs), 36
Shulgin, Alexander, 19
sleeplessness, 30
stimulant, 9, 10, 34, 45

T

techno music, 24

U

underground laboratories, 26–27

V

vision distortion, 30

About the Authors

Lanie Kimlan is a writer living in Washington, D.C. When not writing, Kimlan likes to get away from the city on trips to Appalachia with her golden retrievers, Reeves and Ervin.

Anne Alvergue is a writer and video editor and producer. She has taught in middle schools and at the college level. Alvergue lives in San Francisco.

Photo Credits

Cover, pp. 1, 7, 18, 28, 39, 48, 56, 58, 61, 62 © www.istockphoto. com/FotografiaBasica; pp. 5, 23 Michael Tullberg/Getty Images; pp. 8–9 U.S. Drug Enforcement Administration; p. 11 Hemera/ Thinkstock; pp. 14–15 Digital Vision/Photodisc/Getty Images; pp. 20–21 Brian Snyder/Reuters/Landov; p. 27 MCT/Newscom; pp. 29, 33, 47, 51 Shutterstock.com; p. 37 Doug Menuez/Photodisc/ Thinkstock; p. 40 Image Source/Getty Images; p. 44 Taxi/Getty Images; p. 49 Justin Pumfrey/Taxi/Getty Images; pp. 52–53 Zigy Kaluzny/Stone/Getty Images.

Photo Researcher: Peter Tomlinson